Honeybees

By Myrl Shireman
Illustrated By Pat St. Onge

COPYRIGHT © 2006 Mark Twain Media, Inc.

ISBN 1-58037-356-9

Printing No. D04114

Mark Twain Media, Inc., Publishers
Distributed by Carson-Dellosa Publishing Company, Inc.

Level 3: Book 6

Have you ever heard the buzzing sound of a honeybee? The best place to see a honeybee is near flowers that have blue or yellow blossoms. If you watch closely, you will see the honeybee zipping from flower to flower. The honeybee is looking for flowers with sweet **nectar**. The honeybee will take the nectar from the flowers back to the **hive** where the bee lives. There in the hive, the nectar will be made into honey.

The best place to see a honeybee is near flowers that have blue or yellow blossoms.

4

While the honeybee is in the flower blossom getting the nectar, **pollen** falls on the honeybee. Pollen is a sticky, yellow substance. When the honeybee goes into the blossoms of the next flower, some of the pollen the bee is carrying rubs off on the blossoms of that flower. The pollen carried from one plant to the next helps the plants to make more plants.

Honeybees are often found around fruit trees that are blooming. Because honeybees spread pollen from blossom to blossom, orchard farmers are very happy to see swarms of bees around the fruit trees. As the bees go from tree to tree, they are spreading pollen, and this will make the fruit trees produce more fruit.

As honeybees fly from blossom to blossom looking for nectar, they are spreading pollen.

7

After collecting the nectar and depositing the pollen, the honeybee flies back to the hive. Inside the honeybee's body, the nectar is turned into honey. The sweet honey is the food for honeybees. The honeybee then places the honey in the honeycomb. The **honeycomb** is made of wax. It is made up of many six-sided cells like the picture at the bottom of the page.

In the hive where the honey is stored, there are many other honeybees. The honeybees that fly from flower to flower and tree to tree to collect nectar are female **worker bees**. A very important female bee is the **queen bee**. The queen bee stays in the hive and lays eggs that will become honeybees.

Can you imagine never leaving your home? The male bees who live in the hive are called **drones**. Drones have no sting and gather no honey. The drones and the queen bee never leave the hive. It is the female worker bee you see zipping from flower to flower looking for nectar to make honey.

Today, there are people called **beekeepers**, who build hives where bees deposit nectar. The bees that live in each hive are called a **colony**.

Beekeepers use special clothing
and tools to handle bees safely.

14

The beekeeper collects the honey and places the honey in jars. Some of the honey collected from the hives may be eaten by the beekeeper's family, but much of the honey is sold. The honey that you buy in a store was collected from a hive.

Honeybees spread pollen and provide us with honey. They are very important insects.